THE ROYAL NAVY IN FOCUS 1940-49

£4.50

EDITORS NOTES

When we produced the 1930's edition of this book we had no idea there was so much interest in the Navy of yesterday. What magnificent old warriors were photographed in that edition. Even a quick glance through will delight the enthusiast—and doubtless bring back many a memory to those who were in the Navy at that time. When comparing the Navy of this era—and that which we have today—it hardly seems possible that all the changes we see have taken place in just one generation.

In this second edition we have once again collected together a portfolio from the famous Wright and Logan collection as a representative look at the Navy during the decade. We have deliberately included the old warships that would have been scrapped had it not been for the war. As can be seen, many vessels long past their prime, were retained in the Fleet and served alongside much more modern ships—with distinction. As requested by our readers we have added a "potted history" for each of the ships we have selected for this book. Many make most interesting reading. We are most grateful for the research assistance in this area given by Mr. Bob Todd of the National Maritime Museum.

Whilst the "old timers" mutter "Ah, those were the days" as they turn these pages we youngsters can only sit back and take our hats off to the matelots of yesterday who went to sea—and fought a war—in some ships that we would think twice about crossing the Channel in today!

Most of the photographs are dated on each page after the ships name—you will see that most are post World War II. Photography was seriously curtailed during the war both for security reasons and for the lack of silver needed for the production of both photographic film and plates. We trust you enjoy this second collection of historic photographs and derive as much pleasure in them as we have in selecting them for you.

Mike Critchley
Liskeard
Cornwall

HMS AFFRAY (January 48)

Launched 20.4.45, completed 1946. Lost with all hands in the English Channel 17.4.51. A fracture in her snort mast was officially the cause, but doubt still exists as to the true reason.

HMS AGINCOURT (May 49)

Launched 29.1.45 and completed 25.6.47. Joined the 4th Destroyer Flotilla, Home Fleet, which later became the 4th Destroyer Squadron on general service commissions. Remained in this squadron until 1959 then paid off for conversion to Fleet Radar Picket. Recommissioned 5.62 and served in Home and Mediterranean waters until entering reserve at Portsmouth in 10.66. 27.10.74 arrived at Sunderland to be broken up.

'HMS ALLIANCE (September 47)

Launched 28.7.45 and completed 14.5.47. From 9.10.47 to 8.11.47 she carried out an underwater passage, using only her snort for air, and covered 3,193 miles before surfacing. In 1981 she was opened to the public at

HMS ANDREW (September 49)

Launched 6.4.46 and completed 16.3.48. In May 1953 she made the first ever submerged crossing of the Atlantic, snorting for over 2,500 miles. She was the last British submarine to carry a deck gun. Broken up in 1977.

HMS ANSON (29 July 46)

Launched 24.2.40 and completed 22.6.42. 9.42-3.45 in Home Fleet escorting convoys to Russia and carrying out attacks on enemy shipping off Norway. 4.45 left Home waters for the British Pacific Fleet, returning in mid-1946. She arrived at Portsmouth on 29 July 1946 (see photo). Joined the Training Squadron and was Flagship (1948-49) until paid off into reserve in the Gareloch 17.12.57 arrived at Faslane to be broken up.

HMS ARGONAUT (June 46)

Launched 6.9.41 and completed 8.8.42. After one convoy run to North Russia was transferred to the Mediterranean for the North Africa landings. Night of 1/2.12.42 with other ships of Force Q sank 4 supply ships and a destroyer north of Tunis. 14.12.42 hit by 2 torpedoes from Italian S/M MOCENIGO, bow and stern blown off. Repairs until 4.44. 6.6.44 support ship for D-Day. 15.8.44 invasion of South France. 12.44 joined British Pacific Fleet for operations against Japan. Returned to Portsmouth 6.6.46 (see photo) and paid off into reserve.

HMS ARTEMIS (December 49)

Launched 26.8.46 and completed 15.8.47. On 1 July 1971 she sank whilst alongside at Fort Blockhouse when water flooded through an open hatch when her fuel tanks were being filled with salt water. Three men were trapped in a forward compartment for several hours before being rescued. 6.7.71 raised by R.M.A.S. GOLDENEYE and KINLOSS. 1972 sold to H. Pounds at Portsmouth to be broken up.

HMS AURIGA (October 48)

Launched 29.3.45 and completed 12.1.46. Shown entering Portsmouth to pay off for refit: 12.2.70 during exercises off Gibraltar there was a battery explosion forward and 10 ratings were injured. Broken up 1...

HMS AURORA (February 48)

Launched at Portsmouth 20.8.36 and completed 11.37. Flagship of Commodore Home Fleet Destroyers until November 1939 then transferred to 2nd Cruiser Squadron. Operations off Norway Feb-May 1940. Home Waters until Oct. 1941. Sank German supply ship BELCHEN in Denmark Strait on 3.6.41 with assistance from HMS KENYA. In Force K based on Malta until March 1942. Damaged by mine 19.12.41 off Libyan coast. Repairs at Malta and Liverpool until 7.42. Took active part in invasions of North Africa, Sicily, Italy, the Aegean Islands, & Southern France. Damaged by bomb in the Aegean 30.10.43 and suffered 46 killed and wounded. Under repair at Taranto until 4.44. 17.4.46 arrived at Portsmouth to pay off. Refitted for transfer to Nationalist China. Transferred 6.48. Renamed CHUNGKING. Defected to Communist China 2.49 and renamed TCHOUNKING. 3.49 bombed and sunk in Taku harbour. 1951 Salvaged and recommissioned. 1958 became a harbour hulk.

HMS BAMBOROUGH CASTLE (July 46)

Launched 11.1.44 and completed 30.5.44. As a member of the 8th Escort Group she escorted a number of convoys to North Russia and on 9.12.44 she sank the German U387 in the Arctic while escorting convoy RA 62

HMS BANFF (December 45)

Launched 12.4.30 as the United States Coastguard cutter SARANAC. Transferred to the Royal Navy on lend-lease 30.4.41 and renamed BANFF. Was part of the escort forces involved in Operation Torch, the North Africa landings, in 11.42, and for Operation Husky, the invasion of Sicily in 7.43. In 1944-45 was operating on escort duties in the Indian Ocean. On 27.2.46 was returned to the United States and renamed SEBEC and then TAMPA

HMS BARFLEUR (October 46)

Launched 1.11.43 and completed 14.9.44. Joined the British Pacific Fleet and present at the signing of the surrender document by Japan in Tokyo Bay on 2.9.45. Became part of the 19th Destroyer Flotilla in the Far East. Returned to Portsmouth 10.46 and Paid off into reserve. (See photo) 1953 joined 3rd Destroyer Squadron and

HMS BARROSA (June 47)

Launched 17.1.45 and completed 14.2.47 for service in the 4th Destroyer Flotilla and 4th Destroyer Squadron until 1959 except for two short periods in reserve. 15.3.59 damaged in collision with HMS CORUNNA in the Bay of Biscay. 1959—62 converted to Fleet Radar Picket at Devonport. 1962—66 and 67—68 in the Far East; 1966—67 in Home Waters. Paid off 12.68 at Devonport. In 1971 moved to Portsmouth and used as stores hulk.

HMS BELFAST (October 47)

Launched 17.3.38 and commissioned 5.8.39. 9.10.39 captured German Liner CAP NORTE. 21.11.39 nearly sunk by German mine in Firth of Forth: out of service for three years. 26.12.43 took part in Battle of North Cape — the sinking of the SCHARNHORST. 6.6.44 Flagship of Commander Force E at Normandy. 9.45—9.47 in Far East, returning to Portsmouth on 15.10.47. Recommissioned 15.10.48 for the Far East until 1952. Reserve 1952—56, refit 1956—59, Far East 1959—62, Home Fleet 1962—3, 1963—71 reserve. 2.9.71 left Portsmouth under tow for the Thames. 14.10.71 arrived at the Pool of London after docking at North Woolwich

HMS BEN LOMOND (October 48)

Launched 24.4.45 as LST 3013 but completed as LST(Q) 2 (a headquarters landing ship). Renamed BEN LOMOND in 1947 and operated as headquarters ship for bacteriological defence trials. Broken up at Grays

HMS BERWICK (November 45)

Launched 30.3.26 and completed 15.2.28. 12.39 1st Cruiser Squadron, Home Fleet. In 3.40 intercepted 2 German blockade runners (WOLFSBURG and URUGUAY) which scuttled themselves. Operations off Norway. Escort for raid on Taranto 11.11.40. Battle of Cape Spartivento 27.11.40 — slight damage. Damaged by German Cruiser ADMIRAL HIPPER 25.12 40 while escorting convoy WS.5A in Atlantic. Convoys to Russia and Arctic patrols 6.41 — 6.45 when she began trooping duties from Portsmouth to Far East until 6.46 then in reserve.

HMS BICESTER (March 49)

Launched 5.9.41 and completed 9.5.42. Operated in Mediterranean including (8.42) 'Pedestal' convoy to Malta, 11.42 Operation Torch-invasion of North Africa, 23.2.43 with LAMERTON and WHEATLAND sank U443 off Algiers, 7.43 Operation Husky-invasion of Sicily, 15.8.44 Operation Dragoon-landings in South France. Returned to the U.K. 4.12.45 after service in the Indian Ocean. 1946–50 leader of Nore Destroyer Flotilla then in reserve

HMS BIRCH (February 46)

Minesweeping trawler completed in April 1940. Sold for mercantile use in May 1947. Broken up in 1962.

HMS BIRMINGHAM (June 46)

Launched in 1936, completed 11.37. China Station until 1.40 then 18th CS Home Fleet. Home Fleet until 6.41 then escorted convoy to Durban and became Flagship of C in C South Atlantic until 2.42 when she joined 4th CS Eastern Fleet. Detached for Operation Vigorous (convoy to Malta) June 1942. Refit and work up in Home Waters 4.11.43. 28.11.43 torpedoed by U407 off Cyrenaica in the Mediterranean while on passage to Eastern Fleet. Repair and refit until January 1945 then 10th CS Home Fleet. After refit at Portsmouth 1946—47 joined 4th CS East Indies. Reconstructed at Portsmouth 1950—52, then joined 5th CS Far East. June 1955 sent to South Atlantic during tension caused by Argentine claims to Antarctic Dependencies. 1956—59 Home and Mediterranean Fleets. Broken up at Inverkeithing 1960.

HMS BLEASDALE (November 48)

Launched 23.7.41 and completed 16.4.42. Operated in Home Waters and took part in the disastrous raid on Dieppe 19.8.42, in the invasion of North France 6.6.44, and in many convoy defence actions in the English Channel and North Sea. After D—Day took a more offensive role attacking German convoys and escorts in the Channel and off Holland. 1946—52 Nore Local Flotilla. 18.4.47 was firing ship that set off the demolition charges set on Heligoland to de-fortify the island. 1952 reserve. 11.9.56 arrived at Blyth to be broken up.

HMS BLENCATHRA (August 46)

Launched 6.8.40 and completed 14.12.40. Initially served on East Coast convoy protection duties and then transferred to the Mediterranean in time for the invasion of Sicily 10.7.43, landings at Salerno 9.9.43, bombardment of Leros 15.11.43. Assisted to sink U450 10.3.44, assisted to sink U223 30.3.44. Returned to the U.K. for the landings in North France 6.6.44 - 9.45. 12.47 Air Training Target ship. 1948 reserve 2.1.57 arrived at Barrow to

HMS BONAVENTURE (May 47)

Launched 27.10.42 as Mercantile CLAN DAVIDSON. Purchased and converted to a depot ship for midget sub-marines (X-craft). Operated in Home Waters until 1945 then transferred to the Pacific. Sold back to her original owners in 1948 and converted back to a cargo liner with her original name CLAN DAVIDSON.

HMS BOXER (September 47)

Launched 12.12.42 and completed 1.8.43 as Tank Landing Ship. Took part in the landings at Salerno 9.9.43. Re-fitted as Fighter Direction Ship in 1944, after having taken part in the landings at Anzio(her last task as an LST). In 1946 was taken in hand at Portsmouth and converted to a Radar Training Ship for plotting & air target duties. At one time carried 16 radar sets 23 W/T transmitters and 26 W/T receivers. By 1956 was reduced to reserve and ar-

HMS BUCHAN NESS (August 46)

Landing craft maintenance ship launched 10.2.45. Built in Vancouver Canada. Paid off into reserve 1950

HMS BULAWAYO (October 48)

German Tanker NORDMARK launched 5.10.37. Used as a German raider replenishment ship during the war. Allocated to Great Britain and arrived at Rosyth 8.6.45. 1.46 renamed NORTHMARK. 1947 renamed BULAWAYO and arrived at Portsmouth to refit 7.47. Used for oil freighting until 1950 then laid up in reserve until broken up

HMS BUSTLER (June 46)

Launched 4.12.41. The first fleet tug fitted with diesel engines. Used as a fleet, rescue and salvage tug during the war 1947-58 on long-term mercantile charter then as a Royal Fleet Auxiliary tug. Sold 1973.

HMS CADIZ (April 49)

Launched 16.9.44 and completed 12.4.46. Joined 5th Destroyer Flotilla Home Fleet until 1953. 1953—56 in reserve then sold to Pakistan and renamed KHAIBAR 1.2.57. 12.71 sunk during the Indo-Pakistan war

D79

HMS CADMUS (August 46)

Launched 27.5.42. 8.11.42 took part in Operation Torch — landings in North Africa. 10.7.43 Operation Husky — invasion of Sicily. 9.9.43 Operation Avalanche — landings at Salerno. 22.1.44 Operation Shingle — landings at Anzio. Shown above as divisional leader of the 12th Minesweeping Flotilla. Sold in 1950 to the Belgian Navy as

HMS CAVALIER (June 46)

Launched 7.4.44 and completed 22.11.44. She joined the 6th Destroyer Flotilla of the Home Fleet and escorted major warships on attacks against the enemy off Norway and escorted convoys to Russia. In 8.45 she left for the Far East and returned to Portsmouth on 16.6.46 to pay off into reserve (see photo). Laid up until 1955 and then modernised by Thornycroft at Southampton and recommissioned for the 8th Destroyer Squadron in 7.57. Served in the Far East until returning to Portsmouth in May 1963. After a refit she served from 1966 to 1972. Taken over by the HMS Cavalier Trust and now open to the public as a museum ship at Brighton.

HMS CHALLENGER (October 46)

Undocked 1.6.31 at Chatham. Sailed to Portsmouth for final fitting out and completed 15.3.32. Operated with the Home Fleet 1939—42, East Indies and finally the Australia station, ending up in Hong Kong in January 1946. Returned to Portsmouth 3.46. 1947 Persian Gulf, 1950 West Indies, 1951 Far East. Returned to the U.K. on

HMS CHAMOIS (March 47)

Launched 26.10.42 and completed 22.10.43. American-built Fleet minesweeper. Operated as a danlayer during the invasion of Normandy in 6.44. On 21.7.44 off Normandy was badly damaged by a very close mine explosion and was written off as a constructive total loss. After the war she was sold for mercantile service as the MORNING STAR but the conversion was abandoned and she was scrapped. Shown laid up at Portsmouth in a

HMS CHEVIOT (December 45)

Launched 2.5.44 and completed 11.12.45. Commissioned 12.45 as divisional leader of 14th Destroyer Flotilla for service in the Mediterranean (see photo). 1956-59 8th Destroyer Squadron in Far East. 1960 Harbour training ship for HMS CALEDONIA at Rosyth. 22.10.62 arrived Inverkeithing to be broken up.

HMS CLEOPATRA (September 48)

Launched 27.3.40 and completed 5.12.41. 15th Cruiser Squadron in the Mediterranean. 11.12.42 damaged by a bomb at Malta. 22.3.42 Second Battle of Sirte against strong Italian force during passage of convoy MW. 10 to Malta. 13.12.42 with others sank 3 enemy supply ships off N. Africa. 7.43 invasion of Sicily. 16.7.43 damaged by torpedo from Italian S/M DANDOLO — out of action until 4.45. 6.45 — 1.46 5th Cruiser Squadron, East Indies Fleet. 7.2.46 arrived back at Portsmouth. Home Fleet until 1951 then Mediterranean until 2.53. 15.6.53 Coronation Review at Spithead. 9.54 laid up at Portsmouth. 15.12.58 arrived at Newport to be broken up.

HMS COMUS (August 46)

Launched 14.3.45 and completed 8.7.46. After trials and work-up joined the 8th Destroyer Squadron in the Far East, based principally in Hong Kong. Served throughout the Korean War and remained in the Far East until

HMS CONCORD (January 47)

Launched 14.5.45 as CORSO, renamed CONCORD in 6.46 and completed 20.12.46. Joined the 8th Destroyer Squadron in the Far East and remained in the Far East until paid off in 1957. Served throughout the Korean War. In 1957 was attached to HMS CALEDONIA at Rosyth as static harbour training ship. 22.10.62 arrived at

HMS COTTEL (March 46)

Launched 23.12.41 and completed 12.1.43 (as MMS 142). Renamed COTTEL in 1943 and served as danlayer in the 130th MMS Flotilla based on Plymouth 1943—45. At Lowestoft in 1946 and paid off for sale in November

HMS COWDRAY (October 48)

Launched 22.7.41 and completed 29.7.42. Known to have taken part in Operation Torch — the landings in North Africa 8.11.42. In the Far East in 1945 and returned to Chatham on 5.12.45. 1946 —49 in Nore Destroyer Flotilla.

HMS CREOLE (November 46)

Launched 22.11.45 and completed 14.10.46, joining the 4th Escort Flotilla. Later joined the 3rd Training Squadron based on Londonderry. Paid off in 1953 and sold to Pakistan in 1956. Transferred to Pakistan after re-fit (at Southampton) on 20.6.58 and renamed ALAMGIR. Still in service 1983.

HMS CROSSBOW (March 48)

Launched 20.12.45 and completed 4.3.48. 6th Destroyer Flotilla (later Squadron) until 1955 then placed in reserve. Converted to Fleet Radar Picket at Chatham and recommissioned 4.59. Served in Home and Mediterranean waters until 1963 when paid off at Chatham. Towed to Portsmouth 11.12.63. 1966 harbour training ship

CT 101 (March 47)

Controlled Target boat completed 11.11.47. Renumbered CT 8101 in July 1949. Sold out of service 22.10.1958. Shown running from Portsmouth during lengthy period of first-of-class trials. Built by J.S. White of Cowes.

HMS CYGNET (February 46)

Launched 28.7.42 and completed 1.12.42. Joined the 2nd Support Group on convoy escort and anti U—boat duties. Transferred to the Mediterranean for the invasion of Sicily 7.43. Back in the North Atlantic as a member of the 7th Support Group she, with CRANE, sank U962 on 8.4.44. She was then transferred to the 8th Escort Group to escort convoys to Russia for the rest of the war. Broken up in 1956 at Rosyth

HMS DEEPWATER (June 46)

Former German seaplane tender launched in 1939, and named WALTER HOLTZAPFEL. Seized 8.45 and operated as a diving tender attached to HMS VERNON under the new name of DEEPWATER. By 1952 had been relegated to harbour service and by 1956 was an alongside diving instruction tender moored permanently at HMS VERNON. Arrived at Northam (Southampton) 13.9.60 to be broken up.

HMS DEVONSHIRE (July 49)

Launched 22.10.27 and completed 18.3.29. 26.7.29 17 men killed when gun turret explosion caused fire in the turret. Up to 1939 in the Mediterranean Fleet then, 11.39 Home Fleet. Took part in Dakar operations 9.40. 10.40 — 2.41 South Atlantic. 3.41 — 10.41 Home Fleet. 11.41 — 3.42 South Atlantic. 22.11.41 sank German raider ATLANTIS. 3.42 — 5.43 Eastern Fleet. 5.42 capture of Diego Suarez, Madagascar. 5.43 — 6.45 Home Fleet — refit followed by Arctic patrols and Russian convoys. 1945—46 trooping to Far East. Commissioned 4.47 as Cadet Training Ship. Paid off 10.53. 12.12.54 arrived Newport to be broken up.

HMS DIADEM (January 47)

Launched 26.8.42 and completed 6.1.44. In Home Fleet from completion. Convoys to Russia and anti-shipping actions off Norway 1944—45. Operations in Bay of Biscay 8 — 9. 44. (D—Day bombardment duties throughout 6.44.) In 1948 was Flagship of 2nd Cruiser Squadron. 1950 reserve. Sold 29.2.56 to Pakistan and renamed

HMS DIDO (October 46)

Launched 18.7.39 and completed 30.9.40. Home Fleet until 4.41 then Mediterranean Fleet. 5.41 operations in defence of Crete followed by participation in the evacuation of troops. 29.5.41 damaged by bomb on 'B' gun deck — 46 killed and 38 wounded. Repairs until 11.41. Convoys to Malta including 2nd Battle of Sirte during 1942. 13.12.42 with others sank 3 supply ships off North Africa. 10.7.43 invasion of Sicily followed by operations off Salerno, in the Agean and at Anzio. 15.8.44 Invasion of South France. Joined Home Fleet 10.44. 9.5.45 took the surrender of Copenhagen. Home Fleet until 11.47 then paid off to reserve. 1952-57 Reserve Fleet.

HMS DUKE OF YORK (August 47)

Launched 28.2.40 and completed 4.11.41. 13.12.41 took Winston Churchill to the U.S.A. In Home Fleet on Russian convoy duties until 10.42 then transferred to Force 'H' for North Africa landings. Returned to the Home Fleet late in 1942 and took part in operations off Norway. 26.12.43 played major part in the destruction of the German battlecruiser SCHARNHORST off North Cape. 1944 saw more Russian convoys, followed by a refit. 25.4.45 left U.K. for the British Pacific Fleet. Flagship of the B.P.F. until 6.46 and then Flagship of the C in C Home Fleet 7.49 - 9.51. Flagship of Reserve Fleet 11.51 then moved to the Gareloch to lay up. From 2.58 broken up.

HMS EASTON (September 46)

Launched 11.7.42 and completed 7.12.42. Operated principally in the Mediterranean. 17.2.43 with WHEATLAND sank Italian submarine ASTERIA. 10.7.43 took part in the invasion of Sicily. 22.8.43 with Greek escort Destroyer PINDOS sank U458. 12.44 operating in the Aegean against Greek rebels. 1945—47 in Portsmouth Local Flotilla followed by 3rd Escort Flotilla (Portland). 1949—52 training ship for apprentices at Rosyth. 1953 broken up

HMS ESCAPADE (May 46)

Launched 30.1.34 and completed 3.9.34. 5.12.39 rescued crew of torpedoed SS NAVASOTA in very heavy seas. 4.40 — 6.40 operations off Norway. 6.40 joined Force H at Gibraltar. 23.9.40 operations against Dakar. 30.7.41 escort to fleet air strike against Kirkenes and Petsamo. 6.42 escort of convoy to Malta (Operation Harpoon). By 3.43 converted to destroyer escort and serving in Escort Group B.3 in the North Atlantic protecting convoys. 23.5.43 German S/M U752 scuttled herself on approach of ESCAPADE after being crippled by rocket firing aircraft from HMS ARCHER. 19.9.43 badly damaged during North Atlantic convoy operation (Convoy ONS 18) when Hedgehog prematurely exploded on Forecastle. Sold 29.11.46 and arrived 3.8.47 at Grangemouth to be

HMS EURYALUS (February 47)

Launched 6.6.39 and completed 30.6.41. Joined Mediterranean Fleet until 9.43. 22.3.42 Second Battle of Sirte. 13.12.42 with others sank 3 enemy supply ships off North Africa. 10.7.43 invasion of Sicily. 9.43 Salerno landings. Returned to the Clyde for refit 10.43 — 6.44. Home Fleet untill 12.44 then joined British Pacific Fleet for operations agains Japan. 11.1.47 left Singapore to return to the U.K., arriving at Sheerness 17.2.47. Mediterranean Fleet 1948—53 then South Atlantic Station 3.53 — 8.54. In reserve at Devonport 9.54. 7.59

HMS FAME (February 47)

Launched 28.6.34 and completed 26.4.35. 14.9.39 sank U39 with other ships of the 8th D. F. 4.40 operations off Norway. 16.10.40 ran aground on the Durham coast and severely damaged. Re-entered service 1942 as destroyer escort. 16.10.42 sank U353 while in Escort Group B.6 escorting convoy SC 104. 17.2.43 sank U201. 6.44 joined Support Group 14 for anti-Uboat patrols in the English Channel and Bay of Biscay. 18.6.44 with others of SG 14 sank U767 in the Channel. Served in A/S Training Flotilla post war until sold to Dominica in

HMS FENCER (September 46)

Lend/lease escort carrier used for convoy protection. Launched 4.4.42 and completed 20.2.43 and commissioned 1.3.43. Swordfish aircraft from the FENCER were responsible for the destruction of four Uboats as follows: U666 in the North Atlantic 10.2.44; U277 in the Arctic Ocean 1.5.44; U674 in the Arctic Ocean 2.5.44 and U959 in the Arctic Ocean also on 2.5.44. The last 3 were sunk during the passage of convoy RA 59 from

HMS FLEETWOOD (April 47)

Launched 24.3.36. Served in Home Fleet 1936—7 and East Indies 1938—9. In the Norwegian campaign 4 — 6.40, then served on convoy escort duties. 11.5.43 sank U528 off S.W. Ireland. 1.11.43 with others sank U340 in the Atlantic. Operated as Radio Trials Ship 1947 — 58 based at Portsmouth. Broken up 1959/60.

HMS FORMIDABLE (5th February 46)

Launched 17.8.39 and completed 24.11.40. Joined the Mediterranean Fleet Via the Cape making raids on Italian Somaliland en-route. Took part in the Battle of Matapan 28.3.41. 26.5.41 carried out raid on Scarpanto but severely damaged by German aircraft — repairs in the U.S.A. 1942 in the Indian Ocean. 11.42 covered North African landings. 7.43 invasion of Sicily. 9.43 Salerno. 7 and 8.44 attacks on TIRPITZ. 4.45 joined British Pacific Fleet. 4 and 9.5.45 damaged by Kamikaze aircraft. Returned to the U.K. 5.2.46. 1947—53 reserve. 7.5.53 left

HMS FORT YORK (August 46)

Launched 24.8.41 and completed 27.2.42. Built in Canada. "BANGOR" class minesweeper which took part in the invasion of Normandy 6.44. She was fitted out as a tug for trials with a new type of towed displacement sweep. These sweeps were non-self-propelled barges known as "Egg Crates" and were intended to be towed through shallow waters to detonate pressure mines. These craft were not successful. Sold to Portugal in 1950 as a survey vessel and named COMANDANTE ALMEIDA CARVALHO. Discarded in 1971.

HMS FROBISHER (July 46)

Built at Devonport, launched 1920. Took over 8 years to build. Pre-war served in China and the Mediterranean. 1930—32 converted to training cruiser for cadets and served in this capacity until 1937. In reserve until the war. Refitted and rearmed from October 1939 until January 1942. Served in 4th Cruiser Squadron in the Eastern Fleet until she joined the 1st Cruiser Squadron in the Home Fleet in April 1944. 6 June 1944 bombarded Ouistreham batteries in support of the Normandy landings. Remained in the area until 8 August 1944 when she was hit (forward) by a circling torpedo. Returned to Chatham and then to Rosyth for repair and conversion to a Cadet Training Ship, a role she fulfilled until relieved by DEVONSHIRE. Reduced to reserve at Devonport on 2

HMS GLASGOW (August 47)

Launched 1936, completed 1937. Home Fleet until October 1940. 16 July 1940 in collision with destroyer IMOGEN in the Pentland Firth in thick fog. GLASGOW rescued 120 men from IMOGEN which caught fire and blew up. Mediterranean Fleet until hit by two torpedoes while at anchor in Suda Bay. After temporary repairs joined Eastern Fleet. 9.12.41 sank R.I.N. patrol vessel PRABHAVATI by gunfire (mistook it for Japanese submarine). After refit joined 10th CS Home Fleet. 30.3.43 intercepted German blockade runner REGENSBURG in the Denmark Straight and she scuttled. Rescued 6 survivors. 28.12.43 while operating in the Bay of Biscay with HMS ENTERPRISE intercepted 10 German destroyers/torpedo boats and sank three — T25, T26 and Z27. Operations off Normandy — hit by 2 large shells from shore battery on 26 June 1944. Under repair until 7.45. Post war service in East Indies, America and West Indies, Home Fleet, Mediterranean & Home Fleet before reducing to reserve in November 1956. Broken up at Blyth in 1958.

HMS GLEANER (November 45)

Launched 10.6.37 and completed 30.3.38. Operated as anti-submarine vessel 1940-42. 12.2.40 sank U33 in the Firth of Clyde. 31.8.40 torpedoed and damaged while escorting convoy OA.204. 2 — 5.42 converted to minesweeper at Leith and allocated to 1st M/S Flotilla. Escorted convoys to Russia. 25.8.44 damaged by mine off Normandy — had to be towed home. 14.3.45 damaged in collision with pilot vessel in the North Sea. Based in the north from 10.45 until 6.46 then placed in reserve. Broken up at Preston 1950.

HMS GLENROY (April 46)

Launched as mercantile GLENROY 15.8.38. Requisitioned 21.10.39 as a commissioned transport/store carrier. Converted to an LSI(L) — Large Infantry Landing Ship 1941. Involved in the evacuation of Crete 5.41; the Normandy invasion 6.44 and the assault on Rangoon 5.45. Returned to her owners 8.46.

HMS GLORY (October 49)

Launched 27.11.43 and completed 2.4.45. Sailed for the British Pacific Fleet and joined the 11th Aircraft Carrier Squadron at Sydney but not operational before VJ—Day. The surrender of 139,000 Japanese on the Bismark Islands, New Guinea and the Solomons was signed on board her at Rabaul 6.9.45. 1947 returned from the Far East 1951—53 Korean War service. 1956—61 in reserve at Rosyth. Broken up at Inverkeithing 1961

HMS GORREGAN (September 47)

Isles Class minesweeping trawler launched 30.12.43 and completed 16.6.44. Shown armed with 1 12 pdr and 3

HMS GRENVILLE (April 46)

Launched 12.10.42 and completed 27.5.43. Leader of the U Class (7th Emergency Flotilla). Served in the English Channel and Bay of Biscay during 1943 then sailed to the Mediterranean where she took part in the landings at Anzio. She returned to Home Waters to operate off Normandy (D—Day) and then went east to join the British Pacific Fleet in operations against Japan. During this time was leader of the 25th Destroyer Flotilla. Returned to Portsmouth 4.46 and paid off into reserve. 1951 joined Plymouth Local Flotilla and on 1.10.51 collided with merchant ship ALFGO and lost 7 men. 1953—54 converted to Type 15 frigate. 1983 broken up at Rochester.

HMS HAWKINS (19 May 42)

Launched in 1917 and completed in 1919. Flagship of C in C China station (5th Cruiser Squadron). Sailed for home in 1928. 2nd Cruiser Squadron Atlantic Fleet from 1929 to 1931. East Indies from 1932 to 1935 then reserve at Portsmouth until 1939. South American and South African patrols until December 1941 when she arrived at Portsmouth for a refit which was completed in May 1942. She arrived at Scapa Flow to work up on the 29 May 1942 then joined the Eastern Fleet until March 1944 when she returned home. 6 June 1944 at Normandy landings as a bombardment and depot ship, returning to Rosyth on 31st July 1944. No further service. Reduced to reserve in 1945. Scrapping commenced in 1947 at Dalmuir.

HDML 1406 (1942)

Harbour Defence Motor Launch completed in May 1944 by Newman of Hamworthy, Poole. In 1945 was reclassified as Fast Despatch Boat and given the Number FDB 84. In 1947 was handed over to Nationalist China.

HMS HEDINGHAM CASTLE (May 46)

Launched 30.10.44 and completed 12.2.45 but not commissioned until 12.5.45. Based at Portsmouth for most of her operational career. Present at the 1953 Coronation Review at Spithead. Finally paid off in June 1955 and

HMS HOTSPUR (May 47)

Launched 23.3.36 and completed 29.12.36. During trials on 27.7.36 hit a submerged rock which broke off both propellers. 10.4.40 First Battle of Narvik — 2 German destroyers and 7 merchant ships sunk. 20.10.40 with others sank Italian S/M LAFOLE. 28.3.41 Battle of Cape Matapan. 29.5.41 had to sink HMS IMPERIAL which had been crippled off Crete. 23.12.41 with HASTY sank U.79. 15.6.42 had to sink HASTY which had been crippled in E. Med. 1943 became destroyer escort in the N. Atlantic convoy battles. 6.44 operated in support of Normandy landings. 10.1.48 in A/S Training Flotilla. 23.11.48 to Dominican Navy as TRUJILLO. Deleted 1972.

HMS HOWE (March 46)

Launched 9.4.40 and completed 29.8.42. Home Fleet and convoys to Russia until 5.43 then Force 'H'—invasion of Sicily and Italy. 10.43 refit at Devonport. 30.6.44 left Scapa for Eastern Fleet 2.12.44 hoisted flag of C in C British Pacific Fleet and carried out operations against the Japanese homelands. 8.45 refit at Durban. 9.45-12.45 East Indies Fleet. Returned to UK and arrived Portsmouth 9.1.46. 1946-50 training battleship then laid up at Devonport. 27.5.58 left Devonport under tow for Inverkeithing to be broken up.

HMS ICARUS (April 46)

Launched 26.11.36 and completed 3.5.37. Fitted for minelaying. In 1940 laid mines off Norway. 13.4.40 2nd Battle of Narvik. 31.5.40 damaged by bomb during Dunkirk evacuation. 5.41 escort to HOOD during chase of BISMARK. 1941-42 Home Fleet convoy duties to Russia with detached duty (6.42 and 8.42) for convoys to Malta. 1943-45 destroyer escort to North Atlantic convoys in Support Groups 3 and 4 and Escort Group C.2. 6.44 escort to Normandy convoys. Assisted in the sinking of 4 U-boats during the war—14.10.39 U.45; 29.11.39 U35; 6.3.44

HMS ILLUSTRIOUS (March 47)

Launched 5.4.39 and completed 21.5.40. 9.40 joined Mediterranean Fleet. 11.11.40 21 Swordfish from ILLUSTRIOUS sank one and damaged two Italian battleships in Taranto Harbour. 10.1.41 severely damaged by German aircraft and went to the U.S.A. for repairs. 5.42 covered landings at Diego Suarez, Madagascar. Remained in the Indian Ocean until 1.43 then had 5-month refit. Returned to the Indian Pacific Fleet. 6.4.45 damaged by near miss off Okinawa and hull badly strained. 6.45 - 6.46 refit in UK. 1946-54 Trials and training carrier in the Home Fleet. 3.11.56 arrived at Faslane to be broken up.

HMS IMPLACABLE (May '49)

Launched 10.12.42 and completed 28.8.44. Joined the Home Fleet and carried out raids against shipping off Norway. 6.45 joined the British Pacific Fleet and carried out air strikes against Truk 14 and 15.6.45 and against the Japanese Home Islands 7 and 8.45. 1948-49 refit. 1949-50 Flagship of the Home Fleet. 1951 joined the Training Squadron until 1954 when she paid off into reserve. 3.11.55 arrived at Inverkeithing to be broken up.

HMS INDEFATIGABLE (March 46)

Launched 8.12.41 and completed 3.5.44. Joined the Home Fleet and carried out air strikes against shipping off Norway including the TIRPITZ. 11.44 joined the British Pacific Fleet which was being formed at Trincomalee. Carried out strikes against Palembang, Sakishima, Okinawa and the Japanese Home Islands. 1.4.45 hit by a Kamikaze but the wreckage was swept off the deck and operations continued. 2.9.45 in Tokyo Bay for the signing of the surrender of Japan. Repatriation duties followed by a period in reserve. 1951-54 Training

HMS INDOMITABLE (June 46)

Launched 26.3.40 and completed 10.10.41. 3.11.41 damaged by grounding while working up in the West Indies. 1.42 in the Indian Ocean. 5.42 operations against Madagascar. 12.8.42 badly damaged by German aircraft during Pedestal convoy operation. 7.43 joined Force H for the assault on Sicily. 16.7.43 badly damaged by an aerial torpedo. 7.44 joined Eastern Fleet and in 1.45 transferred to the British Pacific Fleet. 4.5.45 slightly damaged by a Kamikaze but remained operational. 1948-50 extensively refitted and modernised. 1951-52

HMS INGLIS (22 February 46)

Launched 2.11.43, completed 29.12.43 and commissioned 12.1.44 in the Royal Navy (on lend-lease from the USA). She was a short-hulled diesel-electric frigate of the EVARTS type. Escorted convoys in the North

HMS ISLE OF SARK (December 45)

Built in 1932 as a short sea passenger vessel. Hired 22.12.41 for use as a radar training ship and fitted out with various types of radars which were frequently being changed as new types came into use. Note the large

HMS KENYA (October 49)

Launched 18.8.39 and completed 20.8.40. Home Fleet until 3.43, but detached on 3 occasions to escort convoys to Malta. 3.10.41 sank German tanker KOTA PINANG. 27.12.41. raid on Vaagso, helping to destroy 9 German vessels. Convoys to Russia. Night of 12-13.8.42 bow blown off by Torpedo from Italian S/M ALAGI in The Narrows, Mediterranean. Repairs and work-up until 3.43. 4.43 4th Cruiser Squadron, Eastern Fleet. 25.7.44 shelled Japanese shore batteries on Sabang. Supported operations to recapture Burma. Returned to U.K. 6.45 Home and West Indies until 1949. 10.49 left UK for Far East including Korean War. U.K. 1953-56, then cruised to the S. Atlantic, Indian Ocean and Aden before re-joining Home Fleet 11.56. 9.58 paid off into Reserve. 29.10.62

HMS KING GEORGE V (March 46)

Launched 21.2.39 and completed 12.40. 1.41 took Lord Halifax to the USA. 27.5.41 with RODNEY battered the German battleship BISMARCK into a wreck. Took part in convoys to Russia and on 1.5.42 was badly damaged in collision with the destroyer PUNJABI, which she sank. After repairs more convoys to Russia followed until 2.5.43 when she joined Force 'H' for the invasions of Sicily and Italy. After a refit at Liverpool transferred to the British Pacific Fleet and carried out operations, including bombardments, off the Japanese coast. 2.3.46 arrived back at Portsmouth. Flagship of C in C Home Fleet 1946. Training battleship 1947-49. 14.6.50 left Portsmouth in tow for laying up in the Gareloch. 20.1.58 towed to Dalmuir for breaking up. Photo shows her

LCH 243 (September 49)

Built in the USA in 1942 and transferred to the R.N. under Lend/Lease. Formerly an LCI(L)—Large Infantry Landing Craft—and converted into an LCH—Headquarters Landing Craft. Used as a communications headquarters for a group of landing craft. Still in service in 1952. Deleted shortly afterwards.

LCT 4045 (September 47)

Launched 1945. Designed for service in the Far East but the war ended before she was completed. Transferred
to the Canadian Coastguard in 1958 and renamed DAUPHIN. Discarded in 1961.

HMS LEANDER (July 46)

Cruiser launched in 1931 and completed in 1933. 2nd Cruiser Squadron, Home Fleet until 1937 when commissioned for service in the New Zealand Division and represented New Zealand at the Coronation Review in May 1937 at Spithead. Served in Red Sea and Indian Ocean from June 1940 until June 1941. 27 February 1941 sank the Italian raider RAMB I in the Indian Ocean. Joined 7th CS in the Mediterranean in June 1941 then returned to New Zealand in late August 1941. Remained in the South Pacific area until November 1943. Torpedoed by Japanese destroyer during Battle of Kolombangara and severely damaged. Temporary repairs at Auckland until November then permanent repairs at Boston, USA until August 1945. Further refits at Rosyth, Tyne and Portsmouth until August 1946. 1st CS Mediterranean 8.46-12.47. Reserve 1948-49. Arrived Blyth 5.1.50.

HMS LEEDS CASTLE (June 47)

Launched 12.10.43 and completed 15.2.44. Operated on convoy escort duties and patrols against U-Boats.

HMS LIVERPOOL (April 48)

Launched in 1937 and completed in 1938. East Indies, China and Mediterranean until October 1940. 14 October 1940 bow blown off by aerial torpedo from Italian aircraft. Repairs until Feb 1942. Convoys to Russia then escort to convoy from the UK to Malta (Operation Harpoon) during which she was hit by an aerial torpedo and severely damaged S.W. of Sardinia 14th June 1942. Out of service until August 1945. Member of 5th C.S. Med. Fleet from Oct 1945 until May 1952 when she paid off at Port mouth into Category C reserve. Scrapped in 1958.

HMS LOCH FYNE (August 49)

Launched 24.5.44 and completed 9.11.44. Escorted convoys to Gibraltar and in the English Channel. May-June 1945 was escorting surrendered U-boats from Trondheim to Loch Ryan. 8.45-3.46 in the East Indies on patrol duties. Arrived back at Portsmouth 46 and paid off into reserve. Refitted for further service in the Mediterranean and Persian Gulf before finally being put up for sale in 1963. Sold and broken up in 1970.

HMS LOCH KATRINE (2 May 46)

Launched 21.8.44 and completed 29.12.44. Employed on convoy escort and patrol duties. Paid off on return to Portsmouth 2.5.46 (see photo). Purchased in 1948 by New Zealand and transferred after a short refit on 7.7.49 and renamed ROTOITI. Served in the Korean War (carried out 2 tours of duty) 1950-53. Broken up at Hong Kong

HMS LOCH VEYATIE (August 46)

Launched 8.10.45 and completed 13.7.46. The only ship in the Royal Navy to be fitted with the Mark XXI 4" gun. Photo shows her at Portsmouth immediately after completion to carry out proving trials on the gun and mounting. At the 1953 Coronation Review while belonging to the Plymouth Command. Broken up in 1965.

HMS LONDON (September 47)

Launched 14.9.27 and completed 31.1.29. 1929-39 Mediterranean. 3.39-3.41 reconstruction at Chatham then Home Fleet and South Atlantic Service until 3.44. 6.41 intercepted 3 German supply vessels which scuttled themselves — ESSO HAMBURG, EGERLAND & BABITONGA. Russian convoy protection. 3.44-6.49 in Far East and East Indies except for refit at Chatham 1946-47. Actions against the Japanese in the Dutch East Indies and Malaya. 21.4.49 badly damaged by gunfire (23 hits) when trying to rescue the AMETHYST in the Yangtse river -70 dead and 35 wounded. 18.6.49 left Hong Kong for UK to pay off 25.1.50 arrived Barrow to be broken up.

HMS MAIDSTONE (October 48)

Submarine depot ship launched 21.10.37 and completed 5.5.38. Took part in Operation Torch — the invasion of North Africa. Later transferred to the Eastern Fleet. In 1956-58 was flagship of the C in C Home Fleet. Reconstructed at Portsmouth 1958-62. 1969-77 accommodation and prison ship at Belfast. Broken up 1978.

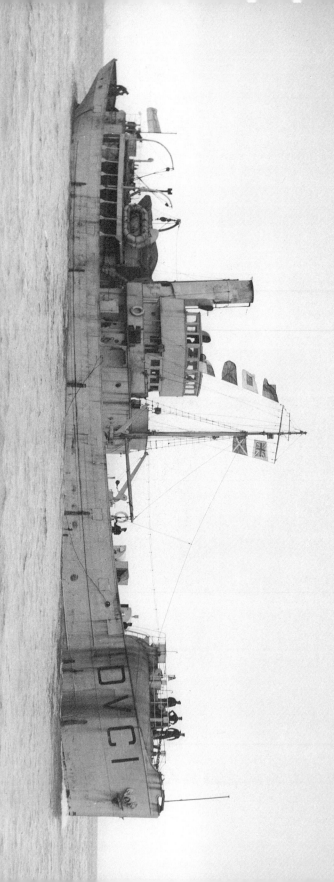

HMS MARIA (April 48)

On 29 May 1941 the German weather observation ship (former trawler) AUGUST WRIEDT was captured in the North Atlantic. She had been built in 1929 and in March 1942 was commissioned into the Royal Navy as a wreck dispersal vessel. She was employed on the demolition of the many wartime wrecks in British coastal waters

MARTINET (August 46)

Launched 8.12.38. Boom defence vessel. Sold 1958.

HMS MATCHLESS (April 46)

Launched 4.9.41 and completed 26.2.42. Served principally in the Home Fleet and on 15.5.42 had to sink HMS TRINIDAD in the Arctic after she had received extensive torpedo and bomb damage. 15.6.42 mined off Malta while escorting 'Harpoon' convoy, repaired and sailed from Malta 12.8.42. In May 1943 was serving in Support Group 4 in the North Atlantic. 26.12.43 assisted in the sinking of SCHARNHORST off North Cape. 1945-46 Mediterranean Fleet. Paid off at Portsmouth 4.46 and reserve until 8.57 when sold to Turkey as KILIC ALI

HMS MAURITIUS (April 48)

Launched 19.7.39 and completed 1.1.41. Until 6.41 escorting convoys to Freetown then moved into the Indian Ocean until 1.42. Returned to East Indies after UK refit and remained there until 6.43. 10.7.43 invasion of Sicily and at 0600 on that day fired her first shots in anger since completing. 9.43 Salerno, 12.43 returned to UK, 1.44 back to the Med. for Anzio landings. 6.44 Invasion of Normandy. 7.44-8.44 attacked German shipping in Bay of Biscay. Remained in Home Waters until refitted between 2.45 and 3.46. Med. Fleet 46-48 then refit at Portsmouth. 30.4.48-3.49. East Indies 5.49-12.51 then refit and reserve at Portsmouth 10.53 until sold for

HMS MENDIP (March 48)

Launched 9.4.40 and completed 12.10.40. 26.7.41 bombarded Dieppe. Home Waters convoy escort until early 1943 then transferred to the Mediterranean for the invasions of Sicily and Italy, including Salerno. 6.6.44 part of the escort for the invasion of Normandy. 20.5.45 entered Harwich reserve. Early 1948 to Portsmouth to refit for loan to China and in 5.48 renamed LIN FU. 15.11.49 sold to Egypt. 31.10.56 captured by Israel and renamed

HMS MINER II (July 48)

Launched 18.8.39 as M2. A controlled minelayer equipped for laying small minefields in coastal waters. In 1942 renamed MINER II. Operated in Home Waters throughout the war. Renamed GOSSAMER in 1949 as a mine location vessel. In 1970 was used as a target for the Iranian destroyer ARTEMIZ (ex HMS SLUYS) and was sunk

ML 106 (1943)

A Fairmile 'A' Type motor launch completed on 5.7.1940. She is shown fitted as a minelayer with the diesel

ML 250 (March 49)

Fairmile 'B' Type motor launch completed on 11.7.1941. Renumbered ML 2250 late in 1949. Sold out of service in 1962. In this photograph she is fitted as a minesweeping motor launch and is armed with 2 single 20mm

ML 6002 (August 49)

Fairmile 'B' Type motor launch completed in May 1941 and numbered ML 223. In 1949 was renumbered ML 6002 for a short time while serving in the British Rhine Flotilla. Later in 1949 renumbered ML 2223 and in 1959 was

MMS 236

Motor minesweeper launched 18.8.42 and completed 29.11.42. Built at Wivenhoe. 132nd MMS Flotilla 1942-45
based on Liverpool (1942-3) and Sheerness (1944-45). 116th MMS Flotilla 1945-46 NW Europe. 102nd MMS
Flotilla 1946 based on Sheerness. At Portsmouth unattached 1947-52. 51st MMS Flotilla 1952-54 based at Port

HMS MODESTE (November 46)

Launched 29.1.44 and completed 9.45 but immediately entered reserve at Chatham until 20.2.46 when she commissioned for service as gunnery training ship based at Portsmouth. Later became tender to VERNON, the torpedo school. 1950-52 in reserve at Portsmouth. 1953 joined 3rd Frigate Squadron in the Far East. 1956 transferred to the Mediterranean. 1958 Portsmouth reserve. 1961-2 broken up.

HMS MORECAMBE BAY (April 49)

Launched 1.11.44 and completed 22.2.46. Part of the Commonwealth Task Force in operations off Korea which commenced in 1950. Sold to Portugal and renamed DON FRANCESCO DE ALMEIA in 1961. Discarded in

MTB 35 (1942)

Built by Vosper at Portsmouth and completed 2.4.41. Operated in the English Channel and made attacks on German vessels off the French coast including one abortive attack on a convoy off Boulogne on the night of

MTB 347 (1940)

Built by Vosper at Portsmouth and completed 18.3.43. Shown running builder's trials in the Solent prior to handing over to the Royal Navy. Sunk, together with MTB 360, when the 11th MTB Flotilla of 5 boats attacked German convoy 1291 on the night of 30 Sept/1st Oct 1944 off Ijmuiden. The convoy was protected by 7 motor

MTB 507 (November 45)

Built by the British Power Boat Co. at Hythe and completed 30.11.45. Renumbered MTB 1507 in 1949. Sold 18

MTB 1027 (December 49)

Completed 28.2.46 as MTB 527. Became MTB 1027 in 1949 and is shown mounting a short 4.5in/8cwt Mk I gun and a twin Oerlikon. Became Fleet Craft 26 (FC 26) in 1952 (harbour service). Sold out of service in January

MTB 2017 (March 47)

Laid down as MGB 517, reclassified MTB 517, then renumbered MTB 2011 in March 1945, again renumbered in May 1945 as MTB 2017 and finally completed 31 January 1946. Renumbered MTB 5517 and sold out of service in

MTB 5036 (December 49)

Completed 22.12.1944 as MTB 794. Renumbered MTB 5036 in 1949. A Modified Fairmile 'D' type boat. Shown fitted as a Gun Boat version with 2 4.5in/8cwt Mk I power operated guns and a twin 20mm Oerlikon mount. Sold

MTB 5516 (August 49)

Laid down as MGB 516, launched as MTB 516. Renumbered MTB 2010 and then MTB 2016 before being completed in July 1945. Renumbered MTR 5516 in 1949 and sold 17th March 1956.

HMS MULL (March 47)

An Isles class trawler launched 27.3.41 and completed 19.8.41. She operated as an anti-submarine escort and on 10 March 1944 she sank U343 off Cagliari in the Western Mediterranean. On 27.4.46 she was transferred to the War Department and was operated first by the Royal Army Service Corps and then by the Royal Corps of

HMS NARVIK (September 48)

Launched 29.7.45 as LST 3044. Renamed NARVIK in 1947. She was flagship of the British Task Force for the atomic bomb tests in the Monte Bello Islands in 1956. Later served as a depot ship in Malta. Broken up 1965.

HMS NELSON (March 46)

Launched 3.9.25 and completed 6.27. In the Atlantic Fleet pre-war. 4.12.39 damaged by magnetic mine off Loch Ewe and out of action until 9.40. 4.6.41 intercepted German supply ship GONZENHEIM in the Atlantic. 7.41 joined Force 'H' at Gibraltar—convoys to Malta. 27.9.41 damaged by aerial torpedo during convoy operations. Escort for 'Pedestal' convoy to Malta 8.42. Invasion of North Africa 11.42. Invasion of Sicily 7.43. Salerno landings 9.43. Invasion of Normandy 6.44. 18.6.44 damaged by mine and refitted in USA, followed by service in the East Indies Fleet. Returned to Portsmouth 11.45 and became Flagship of Rear Admiral Training Battleships. 1948-9 used as bombing target. 1949 broken up at Inverkeithing.

HMS OBEDIENT (August 46)

Launched 30.4.42 and completed 30.10.42. Fitted for minelaying. Served in the Home Fleet during the war. Slightly damaged by gunfire of German heavy cruiser ADMIRAL HIPPER during defence of convoy JW51B in the Arctic 31.12.42. 3.43 was part of the Support Group 3 in the North Atlantic convoy battles. 6.44 part of the covering forces for the D—Day landings. Thereafter mainly employed in Arctic convoys and operations off Norway. In 1946 was Torpedo Training Ship in Portsmouth Local Flotilla. 8.47 in reserve. 19.10.62 arrived at

HMS OCEAN (August 48)

Launched 8.7.44 and completed 30.6.45. Joined the 2nd Aircraft Carrier Squadron of the Mediterranean Fleet and was still in service in 1952 when she saw action in the Korean War. 1954 refitted for service in the Training Squadron. In 1957 was flagship of the Flag Officer Training Squadron, Home Fleet. Went into reserve 1958 and

HMS OCEANWAY (January 46)
Launched 29.12.43 in the United States and transferred to the Royal Navy on Lend/lease. Operated in the

HMS OPPORTUNE (July 46)

Launched 21.1.42 and completed 14.8.42. Fitted for minelaying. Principally attached to the Home Fleet (17th Destroyer Flotilla) for Russian convoy duties and operations off Norway. 9.42 escort to Convoy PQ.18. 26.12.43 assisted in the sinking of the SCHARNHORST off North Cape, June-August 1944 operated in the English Channel in support of the Normandy offensive. Carried out a minelaying operation in the Arctic Sea on 22.4.45. In 1946 was a submarine target ship in the Portsmouth Local Flotilla. Broken up in 1955.

HMS ORSAY (April 48)

Isles class minesweeping trawler launched 1.1.45 and completed 11.5.45. Operated as a danlayer accompanying a flotilla of minesweepers. Sold 1957 as mercantile ANTILOPE. Broken up 1975. Shown armed with

HMS ORWELL (June 47)

Launched 2.4.42 and completed 17.10.42. Fitted for minelaying. Joined 17th D.F. Home Fleet. 31.12.42 Battle of Barents Sea. Detached during 1943 for N. Atlantic convoy support duties as a member of the 3rd Support Group. 6.44 operated in support of the Normandy landings. 22.4.45 laid a minefield in the Arctic Sea. 1946-47 torpedo training in the Portsmouth Local Flotilla, then reserve 1952 converted to Type 16 frigate at Rosyth

HMS PALADIN (July 46)

Launched 11.6.41 and completed 12.12.41. 1942-3 in the Mediterranean - 1944-5 in the Eastern Fleet. Had the following notable successes:- 17.2.43 sank U205. 16.4.43 with PAKENHAM sank Italian torpedo boat CASSIOPEA but then had to sink PAKENHAM because of crippling damaged she had received; 4.5.43 with others 'sank Italian torpedo boat PERSEO; 12.2.44 with PETARD sank Japanese submarine I27 in the Indian Ocean. 1945 48 was a target ship for the 3rd Submarine Flotilla 1952-54 converted to Type 16 frigate. Broken up

HMS PATROLLER (October 46)

Lend/lease escort carrier launched 6.5.43. Used principally as a ferry carrier with a capacity of up to 70 aircraft, depending on type. Fleet Air Arm aircraft for the Eastern and British Pacific Fleets, Royal Air Force aircraft for India and Burma, and USAAF aircraft for the war in Europe were transported. PATROLLER was the last escort carrier to be returned to the US Navy being officially handed back on 13.12.46. She was sold and converted to a

HMS PERSEUS (May 46)

Launched 26.3.44 and completed 19.10.45. Commissioned for service with the British Pacific Fleet and returned to Portsmouth 5.46 to pay off into reserve. Refitted 1949-51. In 1953 was designated a ferry carrier and was present at the Coronation Review in June 1953. Refitted 1955 but placed in reserve. Broken up at Port Glasgow 1958. Photo shows her paying off after her first commission as an Aircraft Maintenance Ship.

HMS PETARD (May 46)

Launched 27.3.41 and completed 15.6.42. Served in the Mediterranean 1942-43 and Indian Ocean 1944. Refit at Portsmouth 8.44-mid 45 then East Indies until returning to Portsmouth 5.46. PETARD is unique in being the only warship of any nationality to have taken part in the destruction of submarines of 3 different countries— German U559 on 30.10.42; Italian UARSCIEK on 15.12.42 and Japanese I.27 on 12.2.44. 1953-55 converted to

HMS PHEASANT (September 46)

Launched 21.12.42 and completed 12.5.43. Operated in the Mediterranean in support of the invasion of Sicily in 7.43 then joined the 7th Support Group for Atlantic escort and anti-U-Boat operations. Escorted part of the invasion forces for the Normandy landings 6.44. By March 1945 was serving in the South-west Pacific as a member of the British Pacific Fleet. Returned to Portsmouth to pay off 9.46 (see photo). Scrapped at Troon

HMS PLOVER (September 46)

Launched 8.6.37 and completed 9.37. Built as a coastal minelayer and on 11.9.39 started to lay mines in the Dover Straits. From 1940 to 1943 operated from the Nore and from 1943 to the end of the war was based at Portsmouth. From 4 to 6.44 was laying a barrage of mines to protect the Normandy invasion convoy routes. Post-war was attached to HMS VERNON and HMS LOCHINVAR for experimental work. Broken up in 1969 at

HMS PLUTO (August 47)

Launched 21.10.44 and completed 1945. Joined the Home Fleet as a member of the 4th Minesweeping Flotilla then transferred to Portsmouth and attached to HMS VERNON torpedo school as an experimental anti-sub-

HMS PRINCESS IRIS (March 46)

Launched 3.8.17 as TRAIN FERRY No. 1. Purchased in 9.40 for conversion, at Southampton, to an LSS (Landing Ship Stern Chute) and named IRIS. Renamed PRINCESS IRIS 1942. Converted back to a train ferry after 6.46 and named ESSEX FERRY. In 1956 renamed ESSEX FERRY II. Broken up at Grays in 1957.

HMS QUEEN (November 45)

Lend/lease escort carrier launched 2.8.43. Did not enter combat service until 1945 and then carried out 4 air strikes in Norwegian Waters between March and May and escorted one convoy (JW.67) to Murmansk and the return convoy (RA.67) to Hvalfjord in May 1945. Used on troop repatriation duties and returned to the US Navy 31.10.46. Subsequently converted into the merchant ship ROERIA!!

HMS RAIDER (June 46)

Launched 1.4.42 and completed 16.11.42. Joined the Mediterranean Fleet and took part in the invasion of Sicily 10.7.43, the assault on Salerno 9.9.43, and the surrender of the Italian Fleet 10.9.43. In January 1944 transferred to the Indian Ocean and shelled Japanese positions in Sumatra and Burma. 6.5.46 Commissioned as tender to aircraft carriers in the Mediterranean. 10.47 to reserve. 9.49 transferred to the Indian Navy as RANA. Placed on

HMS RANEE (November 45)

Lend/lease escort carrier launched 2.6.43. Operated as an aircraft transport ferry carrying up to 70 aircraft on each voyage. These ferrying trips were followed by 15 months on repatriation duties before being handed back

HMS RANPURA (April 46)

Former P and O liner launched 13.9.24. Hired as armed merchant cruiser 6.9.39. Purchased 1943 and converted to heavy repair ship at Portsmouth 1943-45. From 1947 to 49 operated from Rosyth and from 1953-60 in the

HMS RAPID (August 46)

Launched 16.7.42 and completed 20.2.43. After service in the Mediterranean she transferred to the Indian Ocean in 1.44 and carried out support operations, including shore bombardments, against Japanese positions in Sumatra, Burma and the Andaman Islands. 19.3.45 during bombardment of a battery in the Andamans she was hit by a shell and damaged. From 1946 was attendant destroyer to aircraft carriers. 1951-53 converted to Type 15 frigate. In reserve at Portsmouth 1954-1965, then became a seagoing tender to HMS CALEDONIA at Rosyth. 1975 target ship, 1981 sunk as a target by HM S/M ONYX in the Western Approaches.

HMS RECLAIM (June 48)

Launched 12.3.48 and completed in 10.48. Deep diving and submarine rescue vessel operated as tender to HMS VERNON for deep diving experiments. In 1960 was reclassified Mine Countermeasures Support and Diving Trials Ship based on Port Edgar. Replaced by the M/V SEAFORTH CLANSMAN 1978 and placed on the disposal

HMS ROCHESTER (September 46)

Launched 16.7.31 and commissioned 24.3.32 for Africa Station. 1940-44 convoy escort duties, principally in the North Atlantic. 27.3.40 damaged in collision with S.S. LONGFORD. 7.5.41 with other escorts of convoy OB 318 damaged U.94. 19.10.41 with others of convoy HG 74 sank U.204. 6.2.42 with others of convoy OS 18 sank U.82. 31.7.42 with others sank U.213. 15.7.43 with others of convoy OS 51 sank U.135. 31.5.44 damaged in collision with HMS HART. 4.45 tender to Portsmouth Navigation School until 1950. Broken up 1951.

HMS ROYALIST (January 46)

Launched 30.5.42 and completed 10.9.43. Home FLeet and Arctic convoys until 6.44 then transferred to the Mediterranean for invasion of Southern France 8.44. 15.9.43 with TEAZER sank 2 German vessels in the Aegean. 1.5.45 assisted in the capture of Rangoon. 8—9.45 at the surrender of all Japanese forces in the East Indies. During 1945 was the cruiser flagship of the 21st Carrier Squadron. Returned to the UK in January 1946. In reserve until 1955 then refitted and transferred to the Royal New Zealand Navy on loan. Returned to RN

HMS SAINTES (April 47)

Launched 19.7.44 and completed 27.9.46. Fitted with the new Mark VI 4.5in gun mounting in 'B' position (see photo) to evaluate its performance. Attached to Portsmouth for these trials until 1949 when she joined the 3rd Destroyer Flotilla for Mediterranean Service. 1960 joined the 1st Destroyer Squadron for a Home/Mediterranean commission then paid off 4.62, and hulked as tender to the CALEDONIA training

HMS SALVAGE DUKE (November 47)

Launched 1.11.43 as an ocean salvage vessel. Sold to Turkey in 1948 and renamed IMROZ. Lost 14.1.59.

HMS SAVAGE (February 46)

Launched 24.9.42 and completed 8.6.43. Introduced the twin and single 4.5in gun to British destroyers. Operated with the Home Fleet from completion and on 26.12.43 took an active part in the destruction of the SCHARNHORST by carrying out a torpedo attack on her. During 1944-45 operated against targets in Norway and escorted Russian convoys. 9.45—4.47 was gunnery firing ship at Portsmouth. 1950—56 used for various experimental purposes such as the testing of many propellers and shafts. Broken up in 1962 at Newport

HMS SCORPION (September 47)

Launched 15.8.46 and completed 17.9.47 for service in the 6th Destroyer Flotilla (later Squadron) in Home and Mediterranean waters until mid 1956. Paid off for conversion to Fleet Radar Picket at Devonport. 1959—63 in 7th Destroyer Squadron then in reserve at Devonport until 1967, when towed to Rosyth for experimental work to be undertaken on her by the Naval Constructional Research Establishment. 1971 hulk broken up at Bo'ness

HMS SCOTSMAN (September 46)

Launched 18.8.44 and completed 9.12.44. Used by HMS DOLPHIN as a test bed for various hull and casing forms to determine the effect of various projections on underwater speed. Deliberately sunk in early 1964 in Kames Bay as a salvage exercise. After raising was sold and broken up at Troon

HMS SEAFOX (April 47)

Aircraft transport launched 16.5.46. Reclassified as Victualling Store Issue Ship in 1953. Sold 12.58.

HMS SEFTON (June 46)

Launched 23.11.43 as the American CAPE COMORIN, transferred to the Minister of War Transport on completion under the Lend/lease terms and renamed EMPIRE GAUNTLET as a mercantile LSI(L). Transferred to the Royal Navy in 10.44 and renamed SEFTON. Returned to the M.O.W.T. in 9.46 who in turn returned her to

HMS SHEFFIELD (June 46)

Launched in 1936. Completed in August 1937 and joined 2nd Cruiser Squadron Home Fleet. Took part in operations off Norway April—May 1940. August 1940 joined Force H at Gibraltar with RENOWN and ARK ROYAL. Took part in Malta convoy operations and actions against the Italian Fleet. On 26 May 1941 intercepted and shadowed German battleship BISMARK, being attacked by Swordfish aircraft from the ARK ROYAL by mistake! Fortunately no damage was done. 12.6.41 forced German tanker FRIEDRICH BREME to scuttle herself. 11.41 joined Home Fleet. 5.3.42 hit by mine and damaged. Escorted convoys to Russia and North Africa. In action with German cruiser, pocket battleship and destroyers on 31.12.42 and sank the destroyer FRIEDRICH ECKHOLDT. 26.12.43 took part in the sinking of the German battlecruiser SCHARNHORST off North Cape. 7.44—5.45 refit in U.S.A. completed in Portsmouth 5.45—5.46. 8.6.60 became flagship of Reserve Fleet at Portsmouth. 6.1.67 towed from Portsmouth to Rosyth to de-equip. 18.9.67 towed from Rosyth to

HMS SIRDAR (October 48)

Launched 26.3.43 and completed 18.9.43 Part of the 8th Submarine Flotilla in the Eastern Fleet. During 1944 and 1945 she sank six small Japanese vessels and damaged at least one other. Broken up in 1965

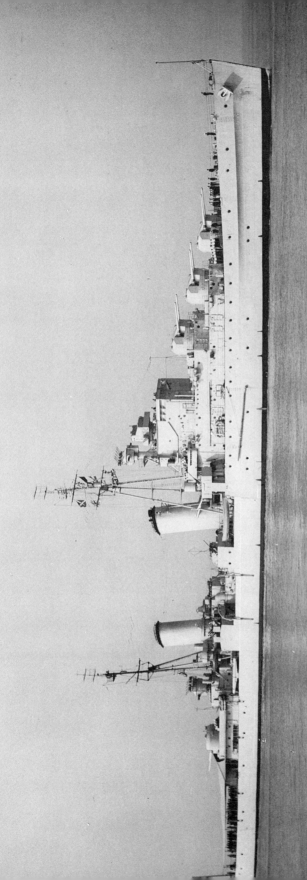

HMS SIRIUS (August 47)

Launched 18.9.40 and completed 6.5.42. Built at Portsmouth Dockyard and adopted by the city. Joined Med. Fleet 12.8.42 'Pedestal' convoy to Malta. 11.42 invasion of North Africa. 2.12.42 with ARGONAUT and others sank 4 supply ships and a destroyer off Skerki Bank. 10.7.43 Invasion of Sicily. 9.43 off Salerno. 17.10.43 damaged by bomb on quarterdeck. Detached from Med. for D-Day landings. 15.8.44 South France landings. Remained in Med. until 4.46 then returned to Portsmouth. Home Fleet until 5.49 then reserve at Portsmouth

HMS SOLENT (June 47)

Launched 8.6.44 and completed 7.9.44. Took part in patrols against Japanese shipping in the Malacca Strait area and assisted the submarine HMS SLEUTH to sink the Auxiliary Minesweeper No. 3 in April 1945. Broken

HMS SPEEDY (April 46)

Minesweeping sloop launched 24.11.38 and completed 7.4.39 1st M/S Flotilla until 6.42. 17.12.41 involved in action with 4 German destroyers in the Arctic—damaged by 4 hits from 5.9" shells. 12.4.42 damaged by ice during Russian convoy. June 1942 escorted "Harpoon" convoy to Malta and then remained at Malta as member of the 17th M/S Flotilla until 8.43. 15.5.43 mined off Malta—12 casualties. Normandy landings. 12.45—4.46 based at Portsmouth 5.11.46 sold and became mercantile SPEEDOM. Broken up 1957

HMS SPORTSMAN (September 47)

Launched 17.4.42. Sank 11 German and Italian merchant ships in the Mediterranean and Aegean during 1943 and 1944. Provided cover for the invasion of Sicily in July 1943. Transferred to the French Navy on loan in 1951 and renamed SIBYLLE. On 23 September 1952 she dived near Cannes—and disappeared. 47 lives were lost and the cause of the tragedy has never been discovered.

HMS STARLING (July 48)

Launched 14.10.42 and completed 1.4.43. The most successful U—boat destroyer of the war commanded by Captain F.J. Walker until his death on 9.7.44. She was leader of the 2nd Support Group and with other vessels was responsible for the following sinkings: 1.6.43 U.202; 4.6.43 U.119; 6.11.43 U226; 31.1.44 U592; 9.2.44 U.238; 9.2.44 U.734; 19.2.44 U.264; 15.3.44 U.653; 29.3.44 U.961; 5.5.44 U.473; 31.7.44 U.333; 6.8.44 U.736; 16.1.45 U.482. In 1946 was disarmed for service as a tender to the Navigation School based at Portsmouth

HMS STATESMAN (July 46)

Launched 14.9.43. Joined the Eastern Fleet based in Ceylon in mid 1944. During 1944 and 1945 sank at least 28 Japanese vessels, principally small sailing craft. Photo shows her after being modified to increase underwater speed and reduce underwater noise. Loaned to the French Navy 1952-59 as SULTANE. Sold in 1961 to H. Pounds at Portsmouth and broken up although the conning tower and casing was intact at the breakers yard in 1983.

HMS STORM (March 47)

Launched 18.5.43. In March 1944 joined the 8th Submarine Flotilla in the Eastern Fleet, based on Ceylon. In April 1944 sank the Japanese minesweeper SOKATEI 7. In the same waters she sank a further 15 vessels,

SUPERB (September 46)

Launched 31.8.43 and completed 16.11.45. 1946-47 Flagship 2nd Cruiser Squadron; 1948 refit and temporary lay-up; 1949-50 Flagship of 2nd C.S. 1951 America & West Indies Station; 1952 Home Fleet and then back to A. & W.I. Station. 1954 Home Fleet as Flag Officer Flotillas Flagship; 1955 A. & W.I.; 1957 C-in-C East Indies. 1958

HMS SUSSEX (February 49)

Launched 22.2.28 and completed 19.3.29. Mediterranean until 10.39 then South Atlantic 12.39. 2.12.39 intercepted German blockade runner WATUSSI which scuttled herself. East Indies to 3.40 then Home Fleet. On night of 17/18.9.40 bombed in dock at Greenock and partially capsized. Repairs until 8.42. 26.2.43 sank German tanker HOHENFRIEDBURG. 3.43—1.49 in Far East and East Indies except for refit at Devonport 9.46—4.47. Returned to Portsmouth 2.2.49 to pay off (see photo) left Portsmouth 26.1.50 in tow for Dalmuir to be broken

HMS SWIFTSURE (August 46)

Launched 4.2.43 and completed 22.6.44. Joined the British Pacific Fleet in operations, including shore bombardments against the Japanese. 8—9.45 one of the force which re-occupied Hong Kong. 1946 Flagship of the 4th Cruiser Squadron. 1951 Flagship of the 2nd C.S. 1953 Flagship of Flag Officer Flotillas Home Fleet. 1955 paid off. 1957 in reserve. 17.10.62 arrived at Inverkeithing to be broken up.

HMS TALLY HO (July 48)

Launched 23.12.42 and completed 11.4.43. Operated with the Eastern Fleet 1943-45 with the following success: 11.43 sank one supply ship of 1914 tons; 11.1.44 sank Japanese cruiser KUMA off Penang; Jan-Feb 1944 sank two supply ships of 4876 tons; 14.2.44 sank German U—boat U-IT.23 off Penang; 7.44 a supply ship damaged; 10.44 sank two small craft; 11.44 sank Japanese small minelayer No.5 and ten small sailing ships. Broken up in

HMS THESEUS (January 49)

Launched 6.7.44 and completed 9.1.46. In the Far East 1949—52 taking part in the early years of the Korean War. 1952 in the 2nd Aircraft Carrier Squadron, Home Fleet. 1954—57 in the Training Squadron of the Home Fleet. 1958 in reserve. 29.5.62 arrived at Inverkeithing to be broken up.

HMS THRASHER (October 45)

Launched 28.11.40 and completed 1941. Fought in the Mediterranean during 1941 and 1942, sank 12 supply ships and the Italian fast sloop DIANA in addition to carrying out supply runs to Malta. On 16.2.42 she attacked a ship off Crete and was heavily counter-attacked. On surfacing, after dark, two bombs were found lodged in the casing. Lieutenant Roberts and Petty Officer Gould removed the bombs at great risk and were each awarded the Victoria Cross. Used to tow one of the midget submarines (X-craft) that attacked the German battleship TIRPITZ in Altafiord, Norway in September 1943. Sold in 1947 and broken up.

HMS THYME (February 46)

Launched 25.7.41 and completed 23.10.41. In May 1942 was part of the escort for the invasion convoy which captured Diego Suarez, Madagascar, from the Vichy French. Paid off at Portsmouth in 2/46 (see photo) and converted to an Ocean Weather Ship and renamed WEATHER REPORTER. In 1947 was renamed WEATHER

K210

HMS TRADEWIND (May, 48)

Launched 11.12.42 and completed 18.10.43. Operated with the Eastern Fleet and on 19.9.44 sank the Japanese supply ship JUNYO MARU of 5065 tons. Was also responsible for the destruction of 7 other vessels in the Indian and Pacific Oceans during 1944 and 1945 but they were mainly junks. Shown after refit in which all external obstructions were removed to increase underwater speed and reduce underwater noise. Broken up

HMS TRENCHANT (April 49)

Launched 24.3.43 and completed 26.2.44 Operated with the Eastern Fleet based firstly on Trincomalee and then Fremantle with the following notable successes: 23.9.44 sank U.859 off Penang; 28.10.44 Chariots from TRENCHANT sank SUMATRA MARU (4859 tons) in Puket harbour; 3.45 with TERRAPIN sank Japanese submarine chaser KUSENTAI 8; 8.6.45 sank Japanese heavy cruiser ASHIGARA in Banka Strait; 8.45 sank

HMS TRIUMPH (May 46)

Launched 2.10.44 and completed 9.4.46. Joined the 2nd Aircraft Carrier Squadron in the Mediterranean as flagship. In 1953 became Officer Cadets Training Ship. 1958-65 converted to a Heavy Repair ship at Portsmouth and was based at Singapore from 1965—72 when she returned and paid off. In reserve at Chatham until 1981

HMS TRUCULENT (May 46)

Launched 12.9.42 and completed 1943. Operated in Home Waters and then in the Eastern Fleet. Had the following notable successes: 4.6.43 sank U308 off the Faeroes: 28.3.44 sank Japanese cargo ship YASUSHIMA MARU (1910 tons) in Malacca Strait; 26.6.44 sank HARUKIKU MARU (3040 tons) in Malacca Strait. 12.1.50 in collision with Swedish vessel DVINA in the Thames Estuary and sank, 57 men lost their lives. Salvaged 14.3.50 and beached; 23.3.50 refloated and towed to Sheerness Dockyard; 8.5.50 sold and broken up.

HMS TUMULT (29 March 46)

Launched 9.11.42 and completed 2.4.43. Joined the Mediterranean Fleet and took part in all the major landings of 1943 and 1944 including Sicily, Italy, Aegean, South France and Adriatic. 29.3.44 with others sank U.223 off Sicily. In 1945 transferred to the British Pacific Fleet (April/May). Returned to Portsmouth in March 1946 to pay off into reserve. Brought out of reserve and converted to Type 16 frigate 1953-54. After serving in the 2nd Training Squadron she was placed in reserve again in 1957. Broken up in 1965.

HMS TURPIN (July 48)

Launched 5.8.44 and completed 18.12.44. Reconstructed at Chatham 1951 with a 12 foot section added amidships to give increased battery power and higher underwater speed. On 9 April 1958 she arrived at Devonport after having been towed from Kingston, Jamaica, by the tug SAMSONIA in 29½ days—the longest tow in British submarine history. Sold to Israel in 1965 and renamed LEVIATHAN.

HMS URSA (March 46)

Launched 22.7.43 and completed 1.3.44. 25th Destroyer Flotilla. Operated off Norway, Normandy (D-Day), in the English Channel (6.44) & the Bay of Biscay. With MAURITIUS and IROQUOIS sank 5 German patrol vessels 22-23.8.44. Transferred to British Pacific Fleet for operations against Japan. Paid off at Portsmouth 3.46.

HMS VANGUARD (May 47)

Launched 30.11.44. Last British battleship built. Photographed leaving Portsmouth for Devonport where she was to be refitted for a Royal Tour which was subsequently cancelled. In 1949 she became flagship of the Home Fleet Training Squadron followed by service in the Mediterranean and Atlantic. Carried out a cruise in the Arctic late in 1952 to test equipment. At Spithead in June 1953 for the Coronation Review of Queen Elizabeth II. After a £1,000,000 refit she went into reserve, first at Devonport and then, from October 1956, at Portsmouth. On 28 November 1956 she became flagship of the Flag Officer Reserve Fleet at Portsmouth, used as a training, accommodation and headquarters ship until she was decommissioned at Portsmouth on 7 June 1960. On 4 August 1960 she left Portsmouth under tow for breakers at Faslane but grounded in the harbour entrance for about an hour. She arrived at Faslane on 9 August 1960 to be broken up.

HMS VENGEANCE (September 49)

Launched 23.2.44 and completed 15.1.45. Served in the British Pacific Fleet in the 11th Aircraft Carrier Squadron but did not see any combat as she was still at Sydney on VJ-Day. Used on repatriation duties, then training carrier with the Home Fleet. Loaned to the Royal Australian Navy 11.52-8.55. 14.12.56 sold to Brazil and extensively modernised in Rotterdam, commissioning on 6.12.60 as the MINAS GERAIS. Still in service 1983.

HMS VESUVIUS (March 47)

Minelaying tender built at Portsmouth and launched 15.11.32 as SKYLARK. Attached to HMS VERNON. Renamed VERNON 9.12.38; renamed VESUVIUS 4.41. Discarded 1956, sold 5.7.57 and broken up at

HMS VICTORIOUS (October 45)

Launched 14.9.39 and completed 15.5.41. Was still working up when her pilots attacked and slightly damaged the BISMARCK during the night of 24-25.5.41. Remained in Home Fleet until 6.44, carrying out raids against TIRPITZ and the German convoy traffic in Norwegian waters. Detached for the Pedestal convoy to Malta 8.42 and Operation Torch 11.42. 7.44 joined Eastern Fleet and 12.44 transferred to British Pacific Fleet. 9.5.45 hit by two Kamikazes but remained operational. 1950-58 completely reconstructed at Portsmouth. 11.67 damaged by a minor fire on board whilst at Portsmouth, but paid off as being uneconomic to repair. 7.70 arrived at Faslane

HMS WAGER (January 46)

Launched 1.11.43 and completed 14.4.44. Joined the 27th Destroyer Flotilla in the Eastern Fleet and took part in a raid on the Nicobar Islands in 10.44. In 11.44 joined the British Pacific Fleet and left Trincomalee on 16.1.45, arriving at Fremantle 4.2.45. Supported the B.P.F. in attacks on the Japanese inner islands and homelands. 1.46-11.47 Portsmouth reserve, 12.47 sailed to Simonstown for reserve th__e __until 1955. Sold to Yugoslavia and

HMS WARRIOR (March 46)

Launched 20.5.44 and completed 24.1.46. Lent to the Royal Canadian Navy 1946-48. Trooping duties to the Far East 1950-51. In 1957 was headquarters ship for the atom bomb tests on Christmas Island. In 7.58 was sold to Argentina and sailed from Portsmouth 10.12.58. 26.1.59 commissioned at Puerto Belgrano as the INDEPENDENCIA. Withdrawn from service and placed

HMS WARSPITE (April 47) with ST. MELLONS and EMPIRE CHARLES

Launched 26.11.13 and commissioned 5.4.15. In 5th Battle Squadron of Grand Fleet in 1st World War. 1924-26, 1933-37 major refits at Portsmouth. 13.4.40 Second Battle of Narvik—8 German destroyers and 1 U-boat sunk. 9.7.40 Battle of Calabria. 28.3.41 Battle of Matapan in which 3 Italian cruisers and 2 destroyers were sunk. 16.9.43 hit by glider-bomb off Salerno and badly damaged. 6.44 bombardment off Normandy and 13.6.44 damaged by mine. 1.11.44 bombardment of Walcheren. In 1946 was sold for breaking up on the Clyde. April 1947 left in tow for the Clyde 20.4.47 tow parted. 23.4.47 drove ashore in Prussia Cove, Cornwall. Wreck even

HMS WEAR (August 46)

Launched 1.6.42 and completed 24.10.42. Operated as a convoy escort in the North Atlantic as a member of the 1st Support Group. Paid off at Portsmouth 8.46 (see photo) and laid up. Broken up at Sunderland 1957-58.

HMS WIDEMOUTH BAY (July 49)

Launched 19.10.44 and completed 13.4.45. Intended for service with the British Pacific Fleet but the war ended before she reached Eastern waters. Arrived at Blyth in 11.57 to be broken up

HMS WOLFE (November 47)

(Former Canadian Pacific liner), launched 3.7.20. Originally named MONTCALM. Requisitioned as an armed merchant cruiser in 1939. Purchased in 1942 and converted into a submarine depot ship. 1946-47 Flagship of

HMS WOODBRIDGE HAVEN (July 47)

Former frigate launched 13.1.45 and converted to a submarine depot and target ship before completion. Completed 19.10.45. 1955-63 used as headquarters ship for minesweepers in the Mediterranean and Far East. Paid

HMS WREN (July 46)

Launched 11.8.42 and completed 4.2.43. Joined the 2nd Support Group under the leadership of Captain F.J. Walker in STARLING. With others was responsible for the destruction of four U-boats—24.6.43 U-449; 30.7.43

HMS ZEPHYR (November 49)

Launched 15.7.43 and completed 6.9.44. Joined 2nd Destroyer Flotilla, Home Fleet and operated against German shipping off Norway. 31.12.44 was torpedoed by U-1020 off Scapa Flow and damaged. Escorted convoy to Russia in April 1945 and was one of the first Allied ships to enter Copenhagen (9 May) after the German surrender. 1946-47 in 4th Destroyer Flotilla Home Fleet. 7.47-2.48 Gunnery training ship in Portsmouth Flotilla, then Leader of the 2nd Training Flotilla in Portsmouth reserve 1954-58. Broken up at Dunston from 7.58

HMS ZODIAC (March 49)

Launched 11.3.44 and completed 23.10.44. Joined 2nd Destroyer Flotilla Home Fleet and took part in operations off Norway and in escorting Russian convoy. At Copenhagen 9.5.45 then to Kiel. 1946 4th Destroyer Flotilla Home Fleet. 1947-48 in reserve then (1949) 2nd Training Flotilla. 1952 reserve. 1955 sold to Israel and re-

INDEX